AF575349

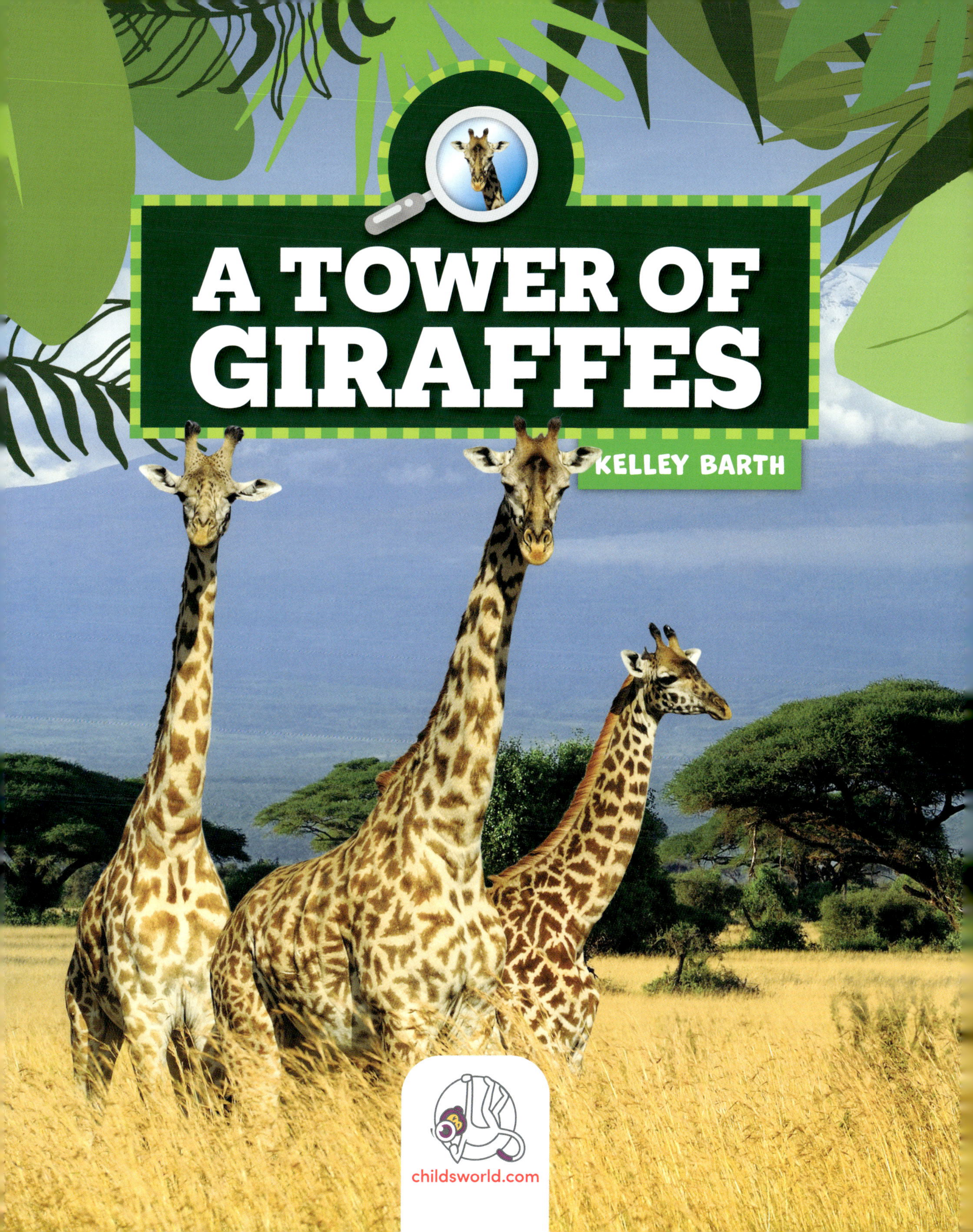
A TOWER OF GIRAFFES
KELLEY BARTH
childsworld.com

Published by The Child's World®
800-599-READ • www.childsworld.com

Photography Credits
page 1: ©Volodymyr Burdiak/Shutterstock; page 1: ©Anastasiia Verych/Shutterstock; page 5: ©Taha Raja/500px/Getty Images; page 10: ©vndrpttn/Getty Images; page 13: ©ZambeziShark/Getty Images; page 14: ©Delbars/Getty Images; page 17: ©Vicki Jauron, Babylon and Beyond Photography/Getty Images; page 19: ©Vicki Jauron, Babylon and Beyond Photography/Getty Images; page 20: ©James Warwick/Getty Images; page 22: ©Dorling Kindersley: Ruth Jenkinson/Getty Images

ISBN Information
9781503884960 (Reinforced Library Binding)
9781503885899 (Portable Document Format)
9781503886537 (Online Multi-user eBook)
9781503887176 (Electronic Publication)

LCCN 2023937303

Printed in the United States of America

Kelley Barth is a former children's librarian who loves connecting with young people over stories and books. When she isn't busy writing, Kelley enjoys reading, hiking, crafting, and exploring national parks. She lives in Minnesota with her husband and dog.

TABLE OF CONTENTS

CHAPTER 1

Meet the Tower

A group of giraffes stands by a **watering hole** on the African **savanna**. They are very tall—a few are even taller than the trees growing nearby. One giraffe uses her long tongue to pick leaves from the very top of a tree. Another is thirsty. She has to lean down very far to drink. She spreads her front legs wide and slowly lowers her head. Suddenly, another giraffe makes a low growling noise. There's danger nearby. She spots a crocodile's head emerging from the water. The giraffe alerts the others to danger. They will find somewhere else to drink.

Giraffes only need to drink water once every few days. They get most of their water from the plants they eat.

Giraffe Size Comparison

The average giraffe is between 14 and 19 feet (4.3–5.8 meters) tall. Giraffes weigh between 1,500 and 4,250 pounds (680–1,930 kilograms).

The average human is between 5 feet 4 inches and 5 feet 9 inches (162–175 centimeters) tall.

A group of giraffes is called a tower. A tower usually has between 10 and 20 giraffes. But there can be up to 70 in a group. Female giraffes live in towers with other female giraffes. Males live either alone or in separate towers.

When female giraffes have babies, they live in towers called nurseries. These towers are made up of several mothers with their babies. In a tower, there are more eyes to look out for **predators**. This helps to keep the babies safe.

TYPES OF GIRAFFES

There are nine different types of giraffes. Each type lives in a different area. Every giraffe has a unique pattern of spots, just like human fingerprints. These spots help giraffes recognize each other. You can tell where a giraffe lives based on its color and spots. All giraffes have long heads with two rounded horns on top. These horns are called **ossicones**, and giraffes are born with them.

Giraffe towers live throughout central, eastern, and southern Africa. They live on hot and dry **plains**. Giraffes spend most of their day eating. One giraffe can eat up to 75 pounds (34 kg) of leaves every day.

A tower travels across large areas to look for food and water. In areas where there is plenty of water, a tower's home range is around 33 square miles (85 square kilometers). In drier areas, giraffes can travel up to 580 square miles (1,500 square km) in search of food.

AFRICA
Atlantic
Ocean
Indian
Ocean
KEY
Where
giraffes live

All in the Family

When a male giraffe is around seven years old, it finds a female that is also ready to **mate**. After 15 months, a baby giraffe is born. Baby giraffes are called calves. Giraffe calves weigh 100 to 150 pounds (45–68 kg). They are already 6 feet (183 cm) tall when they are born.

Mother giraffes give birth standing up. Calves have a long fall to the ground! But they don't get hurt. Calves stand up and run a few hours after being born. During the day, most of the tower goes off in search of food. One giraffe stays behind to babysit the calves. Young giraffes face many dangers. Leopards, hyenas, lions, and crocodiles all eat young giraffes. Only half of giraffe calves survive their first year.

Mother giraffes have one calf at a time.

Who's in Charge?

Towers of giraffes are mostly peaceful. But sometimes, young male giraffes will fight each other. They fight to prove who is in charge. Giraffes fight with their necks. They push their necks into each other. Male giraffes also swing their necks to throw each other off balance. Giraffes even jab each other with their ossicones. When the fight is over, they go back to being peaceful.

Life is dangerous for a tower of giraffes. But they can defend themselves from predators. Giraffes are fast. They can run almost 35 miles (56 km) an hour. It is hard for predators to catch an adult giraffe on the run. Giraffes also have powerful legs and sharp hooves. One kick from a giraffe can kill a lion.

Giraffes' necks are very strong and flexible.

There is safety in numbers! Zebras and giraffes work together to stay safe from predators.

Female calves live with their mothers for a while. But they don't all stay in the same tower for their whole lives. When they are older, some might move on to another tower. Mother giraffes live together. They all take care of the calves. This helps more calves survive.

Strong senses help mother giraffes keep their towers and babies safe. Their senses of smell and hearing are very strong. But vision is their most important sense. Giraffes are one of the only **mammals** that can see multiple colors. They can see far away. They can even see if another animal is sneaking up behind them. It isn't easy to surprise a tower of giraffes. Other animals rely on giraffes for safety, too. Zebras sometimes live near towers of giraffes. When the giraffes warn each other of danger, the zebras can escape as well.

CHAPTER 4

What Makes Towers Unique?

A tower of giraffes is an amazing sight to see! Giraffes are famous for their long necks. A giraffe's neck can be 6 feet (183 cm) long. Even though their necks are so long, they only have seven **vertebrae**. That is the same number of neck bones most mammals have, including humans. Giraffes are tall enough to spot predators from far away.

People once thought giraffes didn't make sounds. But towers do communicate with each other. They make very low humming sounds. These noises are hard for humans to hear. But giraffes can hear each other from more than a mile away! Giraffes also use their bodies to communicate. An angry giraffe may lower its neck to the ground. A giraffe can use body language to warn other giraffes of danger.

GIRAFFE TONGUES

Long necks aren't the only special thing about a tower of giraffes. They also have very long tongues. Giraffes use their tongues to clean their noses and even their ears. Long tongues also help them pull leaves off trees. But a giraffe's tongue isn't pink like most mammals. It is black. This darker color protects the tongue from sunburn.

A giraffe's tongue is 10 to 20 inches (45.72–50.8 cm) long.

CHAPTER 5

Why Towers Matter

Giraffes in a tower help to keep each other safe. They work together to protect calves and watch out for danger. Giraffes are awake most of the day. They do not need a lot of sleep. They are able to lie down, but they usually sleep standing up. This way, they can make a quick escape if danger is near.

Giraffes need to bend down low to reach water. They are unsteady and **vulnerable** when they bend down. Adult giraffes do not have many predators. But lions and crocodiles will attack vulnerable giraffes. The tower keeps an eye out for danger when another giraffe is drinking. Living in a group helps giraffes stay safe.

A lion can run as fast or faster than a giraffe, but one kick from a giraffe can end the chase.

Giraffe towers face many dangers from humans. Giraffes are losing their **habitat** as humans take up more space. People also hunt giraffes for meat and skin. But towers are important to the environment. Giraffes reach food most animals can't. Giraffe towers spread seeds from tall plants and trees that only they can reach. Eating from tall trees also helps sunshine reach lower plants. This creates more food for shorter animals and keeps the environment healthy.

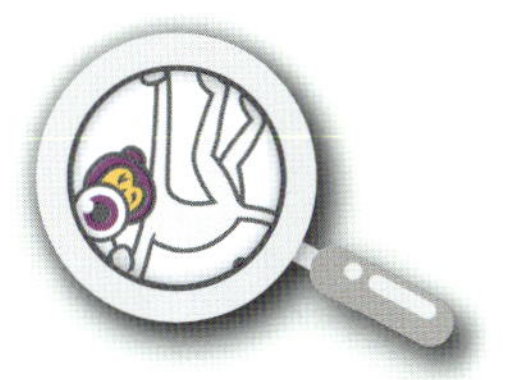

Wonder More

Wondering about New Information

What new information did you learn about giraffe towers? Write down three new facts that you learned. Did this information surprise you? Why or why not?

Wondering How It Matters

Have you ever seen a giraffe before? What would you do if you came across a tower of giraffes in the wild? How can you help protect wild giraffes?

Wondering Why

Giraffes don't always stay with a single tower for their whole lives. What are some of the advantages of this? What are some of the disadvantages?

Ways to Keep Wondering

After reading this book, what questions do you have about giraffe towers? What can you do to learn more about them?

Giraffe Prints

Giraffe spots can be different colors, sizes, and shapes. Every giraffe has a unique pattern of spots, just like your fingerprints.

What You Need:

- Paper
- Markers
- Ink pads or finger paint

Steps to Take:

1. Draw the outline of a giraffe. Look at the pictures in this book if you need help and ideas. Don't forget to add in eyes, ears, mouth, ossicones, a tail, and hooves!

2. Now it is time to give your giraffe its unique spots. One by one, cover your fingerprint in ink or paint and give the giraffe a new spot. Try different fingers until your whole giraffe is spotted.

3. Make sure to wash the ink off your hands!

Glossary

habitat (HAB-uh-tat) A habitat is the place where a plant or animal normally lives.

mammal (MAM-uhl) A mammal is a warm-blooded animal with a backbone. A mammal baby drinks its mother's milk.

mate (MAYT) When animals mate, they join together to produce offspring.

ossicones (OSS-ih-kohnz) Ossicones are another name for a giraffe's horns.

plains (PLAYNZ) Plains are large, relatively flat areas with few trees.

predator (PRED-uh-tur) A predator is an animal that hunts other animals for food.

savanna (suh-VAN-uh) A savanna is a large grassland with few trees.

vertebrae (VUR-tuh-bray) Vertebrae are the bones of the back and neck.

vulnerable (VUHL-nur-uh-bul) Vulnerable animals are open to attack or damage.

watering holes (WAH-tur-ing HOHLZ) Watering holes are places where many animals gather to drink water.

Find Out More

In the Library

Emminizer, Theresa. *Giant Giraffes.* New York, NY: PowerKids Press, 2021.

Gray, Karlin. *Anne and her Tower of Giraffes: The Adventurous Life of the First Giraffologist.* Toronto, ON: Kids Can Press, 2022.

Markle, Sandra. *The Great Giraffe Rescue: Saving the Nubian Giraffes.* Minneapolis, MN: Millbrook Press, 2023.

On the Web

Visit our website for links about giraffe towers:
childsworld.com/links

Note to Parents, Caregivers, Teachers, and Librarians: We routinely verify our web links to make sure they are safe and active sites. So encourage your readers to check them out!

Index